LIFE (AND THE UNIVERSE)

in 52 poems

Roger François Vila

ISBN-13: 9798721801334

Cover design derived from:
- Vitruvian Man (L'uomo vitruviano by Leonardo Da Vinci)
- Galaxy Messier 101, also known as NGC 5457, nicknamed the Pinwheel Galaxy.
ESA/Hubble

Library of Congress Control Number: [ ]

Printed in the UK

This book is dedicated to Wikipedia and to all who have collaborated to make it one of the great achievements of mankind.

10% of all sales whether digital or physical will be donated to the Wikipedia Foundation annually.

Text that is underlined in the ebook will link to the relevant Wikipedia article or other source.

CONTENTS

INTRODUCTION

Douglas Adams, in his Hitch-Hikers Guide to the Galaxy series, famously postulated the *penultimate* question as being "What is the Meaning of Life, The Universe, and Everything?" (to which the answer was "42").

The *ultimate* question was revealed in book 3 of the series as being "What do you get if you multiply six by nine?". The implication being that there is something fundamentally wrong with the Universe, or that it is a giant joke.

For time immemorial people have wondered about the world. Each religious tradition tried to make sense of the world that we live in, to provide the ultimate answers.

If every effect has a cause, but the cause is not known, the effect is a mystery and the cause has to be magical or supernatural.

- To someone who has never seen a weather forecast, each storm or bout of fair weather is a result of direct action from a God or Gods, whom it would be wise to propitiate.

- Without medical knowledge, the difference between life and death is a mystery that can only be explained in terms of a magical spirit or soul, without which the body returns to the 'clay' from which it was made.

- Until the theory of evolution, the very existence of mankind (and indeed of all animals) was a profound mystery. Where do we all come from? These days the answer is straightforward (in principle), but it wasn't always so.

- In this life, things sometimes go wrong. Life can seem so unfair, when even the righteous come to harm without apparent reason. Many religions try to reconcile us to this. For a religious person, living a virtuous life often promises a second, luckier, bite at the cherry or perhaps a heaven to aspire to.

Traditionally the world itself is seen as static.
The Old Testament book of Ecclesiastes spells out the weariness of this static view (verse 9, *"What has been is what will be, / and what has been done is what will be done, / and there is nothing new under the sun."*)

The poems in this book are written from the point of view of a positive or 'strong' atheist who finds comfort in evolution rather than religion, believing that evolution has a direction from simple to complex and from 'OK' to 'better' design. This position does not need the Gods either to have made the world or to provide a hypothetical better world to come. We have the reasonable expectation that one will be evolved.

As an individual, each and every one of us is doomed to die, but we must accept this as our birthright: evolution includes both birth (it spreads individuals) and death (it gives room for future generations).

Since birth and death are what made us and our forebears, to complain about death is like a motorist in the rush hour complaining about all the traffic.

We might as well enjoy the ride while we can - and try to leave some good behind!

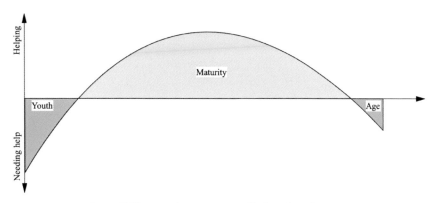

A good life puts in more overall than it takes out.

CHERRY BLOSSOM HAIKU

Cherry nectar skies
Myriad hidden insects gorge...
Feast for eager birds.

THE MIGHTY ATOM

The atom is so titchy small,
That if you took an apple,
And, like Newton in your minds' eye,
Blew it up as big as planet Earth

Then, each atom of your old apple, would itself
Be of apple sized. But not alone
Travel now to centre core.
Around you in all directions
Some eight septillion more....

NB. A septillion (also known as a quadrillion in the 'long' scale) is 10^{24}

Atoms in an apple: https://www.feynmanlectures.caltech.edu/I_01.html

If you are keen you can check whether Feynman was right:
Average radius of the earth 'R' = 6,371,000m
A typical apple has a radius 'r' = 3cm = 0.03m and weighs 100gm (approx.)

Ratio between the radii = R/r = 6,371,000/0.03 = 210,000,000
Ratio between volumes = $(R/r)^3 = 210,000,000^3 = 8 \times 10^{24}$

1gm of hydrogen 'H' has 6×10^{23} atoms (6×10^{23} is known as the Avogadro constant, 'N_A'. The value of N_A was found by Jean Perrin in 1929 by recording 'Brownian motion', the movement of a speck of dust being buffeted by individual atoms of a known amount of gas.)

The same number of atoms of oxygen 'O' weighs 16gm.
The same number of carbon atoms 'C' weighs 12 gm.
Water is H+O+H, weight 18gm per N_A molecules, 3 atoms per molecule.
Carbohydrates are typically C+H+H+O, weight 30gm per N_A molecules, 4 atoms per molecule.
Per 100gm we are told that an apple has 86gm water, 14gm carbohydrate. Per apple therefore there are nearly $5 \times N_A$ molecules of water and $0.5 \times N_A$ molecules of carbohydrate.
ie, $(5 \times 3 + 0.5 \times 4) \times N_A$ atoms, ie 1×10^{25} atoms per 100gm.

So, yes, the numbers more or less match up.

POWERS OF TEN

Some remote tribes it's said of old
Could only count to four, all told
If half a dozen cows should wander through
'A lot' of cows would have to do.

The list of numbers they missed out on
Was nigh infinite and then some
Thousands, millions, trillions more,
When they could only count to four.

The only adds that they could do
Were one and three and two and two.
Put these together and you've got
What these poor tribes would call a lot.

Think how lucky we are able
To recite our ten times table!

*A **lot** of cows!*

Formerly to count a herd such as this the cattle would be driven one by one through a gate. The person standing at the gate would count to twenty, then make a mark on a stick. Hence twenty is known as 'a score'.

These days each cow has an ID tag, which allows exact checks on milk yield etc for each cow. If the milking parlour is automated, food supplements can also be added in to their feed, on a 'per cow' basis.

A SENSE OF WONDER

Ancient tribes had many gods
All around so many mysteries
Wind, rain, earth, fire
Sun, storm, tree, child.

Each imbued by secret magic
Powers from what source?
What made stars wheel in the sky?
.... Forces beyond comprehension.

Each and every thing we've learned
Has moved those magic gods away
Given reasons for the weather
Whence we came and why we are.

Mindful monkeys planet based
In this vast universal space ....

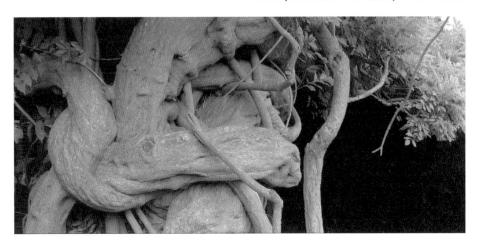

Alive!

OUR WOODWORM LIFE

This woodworm life
We chew away
Digging deeper
Where we lay.
Become lovers,
Share a hole.
Work together,
Spawn and grow.

All the while though,
Our great tree,
Floating downstream,
To the sea.
All unknowing,
Dream and strive,
Slowly sinking,
As we rise.

Grind our teeth down,
Work our way,
Eating, sleeping,
Hope and pray.
Gently rotting,
Through and through,
Us two wood worms,
Me and you.

We can all feel down in the dumps sometimes

WE__STAND__TALL
Together
If we win, it's
Together
If we lose, it's
No matter
Come what may we've
Each other
We are still a team.

THE HOURGLASS

We jostle for the space,
The narrow space
As we grow in hope to follow
Our falling forefathers.

Neck and neck we strive, sharp-elbowed,
To make our mark each day,
Widening the path we all must travel.

Then finally the void.
Our time is up and we are lost,
Beached upon the blanched bones,
Dust of our ancestors.

But behind us our children
And theirs,
Race for the gap.
Full of life - so full of life!

An hourglass does run a little faster the more often it has been used, because the sand becomes finer and the gap slightly wider as the two erode each other. See hourglass.

ACCELERANDO

We were all by nature formed
But nature moves with glacial tread.
Yawning aeons pass unmourned
Alive a day, a long time dead.
The fly that's in the amber buzzing
The same as every fly that's been.

Our speech we learned at mothers knee
By firelight heard the old folks tales
Misremembering monkeys see
Common sense and myth engrailed.

To read and write was the next phase
Learning all there was to know
History and our songs of praise
Placed in context high and low.

Next to science we were called
Prisms rainbowed onto walls
Scalpels sharp the quick to cut
Forces to our wish construct.

Now in each and every hand
All that's known is opened wide
On giant shoulders do we stand
Speak in tongues - no answers hide.
Outer space or fermion dish...
Take a selfie, make a wish.

Rejoice now and grandly grow
Proudly *accelerando.*
Great from cultural evolution -
Citizens of our own creation.

With apologies to the flies.... Flies can evolve quite quickly when their environment changes. Drosophila melanogaster are a favourite with researchers in genetics, because of their rapid life cycle, large number of offspring per generation and convenient size.

Flies however generally stay within a given ecological niche, unlike humans with their runaway cultural evolution.

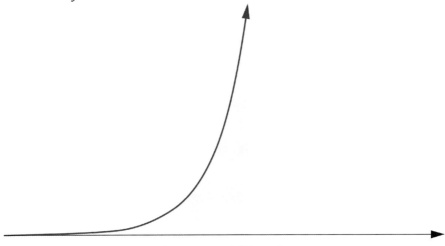

An exponential function

Accelerando by Charles Stross is a lively SF ebook, free

Like torpid porpoises we lie
Basking in the swelling sighs
Of sleep that lap our bodies.
Your neck is cradled in my arm
That you may never drift away.
We float, perchance to dream.

Oftentimes we dive down into the deep.
I proffer my caveman club
You kindly guide me in
To your primeval sea. Now
Chain ourselves to a rock of lust
And gasping fight for breath
Until with a last convulsive shudder
Achieve release.

Back up to the surface sky
Our passion spent, caressing still.

Suddenly I remember
In the Lakes near Wasdale Head
To our left Great Gables' shoulder
All around, a desert land.

Us toiling upwards with light hearts
Our packs upon our backs
To our self-appointed quest.
Pillar by North-West.

Sunshine after rain.
Our path crossed by hill-born water.
Each stone picked out in light.
Things were simpler then.

AT THE DOCTOR'S

The waiting room with rows of seats
Little snapshots full of strangers
Each a story yet to speak
Privately to learned doctor.

On the rotary display stands
Leaflets many, stacked in packs
Listing oh so many ailments
Sound advice we maybe lack.

Mishap joke or tragedy
Who's to know and who's to guess
Sherlock Holmes would have a field day...
Who'll get well and who's a mess.

Speculations all endure
Relief hoped for, and a cure?

...Most of the leaflets have since gone, but the patients remain.
You could look up anatomy for some illustrations...

In the Men's Bar as of right
We would wait the word to hear
Where the party is tonight?
Where to bring our can of cheer.

Ellesmere Road at one 0 four
Terrace long and down at heel
Stepping down to river raw
That's where fate did spin my wheel.

Like some angel Klimt had painted
Breasts on show through satin gauze
Northern accent, pithy wit,
You had much to make me pause.

Lover's course ne'er did run even
Neither quick to bend our will
Though I now be sixty seven
Alma Dear I love you still.

Can be sung to the hymn 'Praise my Soul the King of Heaven'

See Judith_and_the_Head_of_Holofernes

With each poem do we seek
Ultimately the truth to tweak.

Search out the secret alchemy
Burn off the dross, reveal the gold.
From tone to tune, sound to melody,
Narrative to story, and thence to myth.
With subtle skill peel off the old
Unpick the knots that lead to bliss.

If my song with you doth chime
If our heartstrings do entwine
Let truths that touched us new align
Turn phrases magically to rhyme
Reach infinity in a blink of time
Form thoughts subliminal and sublime.

See William Blake's Angel of the Revelation ?

A gossamer trace on the smooth brow of youth
Marks you down as mortal
When barely at full strength.
That first bittersweet pang – it's just the start!
As time's spider reels you in
Binding ever tighter, age upon age.

Now deep fissures on my face
Show to all the very trace
Of times now past, a life once lived.
Ten thousand days and more
Have etched ever deeper those slight lines
And ploughed my brow with furrows
That now are vast as canyons
Eroded by ten thousand suns.

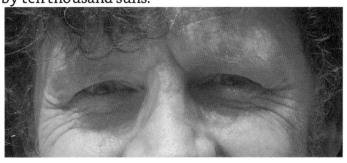

Found a wife, found my life,
Raised two children, gone in a trice.
Greyed my hair and grizzled beard
Turtled eyes look back in tears

Of self-pity? If so, why?
Give thanks I'm old before I die.

WEDDING CAKE

The deal is done, the couple's wed
They'd maybe like to go to bed!
But clear we know the show's just started
The day's now for... the wedding party.

Her mum has spent many long hours
On who to ask, and who wears flowers.
A great-aunt here, three cousins there
Politics of placement with such care.

The wedding cake sits center stage
Marzipan rich, icing made snow
Surface smooth, a virgin page.
Tiers are three, high, middle, low.
[Atop it stands in tiny effigy
The wedding couple, full finery.]
Now speeches long, and maybe witty
Give pride of place to ceremony.
The cake is cut with manly knife
All have their part, for each a slice.

On paper napkins, paper plates
Every share is passed about

The young wolf theirs down at a great pace
For them the cake is just a treat.
The elders wrap their gift away
Their memories for to keep
They're not so keen on wedding cake
A bit too sweet to eat.

WEDDING TAPES

Take two lovers, X and Y
The ribbon of their DNA
May run to ninety years apiece

Let's borrow a little time
From some of their friends
Bundle it into a knot,
Staple firmly, fix safely, X marks the spot.

Anchor to a car or to a kite
The winds of time now buffet both together
Now they're reel to reel

Fast forward....

This poem just shows how quickly technology can become obsolete. Cassette tapes were very common 1970 – 2000 for magnetic storage of music and data. The relatively narrow tape often deteriorated in use and was considered inferior to the larger-format reel to reel tape used by professionals. Old tapes were sometimes fastened to the back bumper of the car that the wedding couple were to drive off in, in a form of harmless practical joke. The tape would unwind into a long stream (reminiscent of the streamers in a ticker-tape parade - even older tech).

THE BRAVE AND HIS SQUAW MAKE LOVE

The dawn mists shimmer over the lake.

Two travellers and their mystic craft
Are now revealed.

No angels these, but lovers
Their boat from prow to stern
Skinned with their seven senses
Over a fine framework of passion.

Each separate element intimately bound
Carries them purposely forward.

A nice canoe that they could have used is made by B.N. Morris of Maine.

IN THE BEGINNING

"In the beginning was simplicity"
So wrote Dawkins, thinking deeply
Truth he told, controversially.
Spelt it out, impressive clarity.

Take Darwinism, add game theory
Genetics multiply with biology
Computer graphics using symmetry
Climbing mountains' improbability.

Step by step but rising gradually
Life's robots lay down geology
From single pathway that was lucky
Building up the great diversity.

So much science, one single vision
Well done Dawkins - jolly well done!

"In the beginning was simplicity" is the opening sentence of "The Selfish Gene". It is a reworking of the first words of the Bible ("In the beginning was the Word...")

The sun-god in his chariot
We know will come back soon
The birth of good in man they wrote
Shall light this hallowed room.

In every new-born child lies hope
To future perfect find
Heaven upon Earth the glorious scope
Of greater humankind.

Let's start our Christmas time in style
At home in house secure
And tarry happy for a while
Then off to stories sure...

Of food and drink and company
At home and out beyond the sea.

France, Japan, Mauritius
They all are waiting just for us
In each shall seek some memories sweet
The whole world's at our wandering feet.

Inside the womb, a lucky break
Unintentionally did make
A single secret cell
On holy mission duly bent

Split and split again
Geometrically progressing
From fish to flesh to foetus
All unknowing nature's art

Now a bulge begins to swell
Inside your living belly
Bump in months forms gravid lump
Affirms the weight of destiny

At last the time has come
Will she nil she now must bear
Down from out her body
The great and alien form.

Tearing open living flesh
To force a chance at life.
At last, relief and wondrous joy
It's a girl! Or, it's a boy!

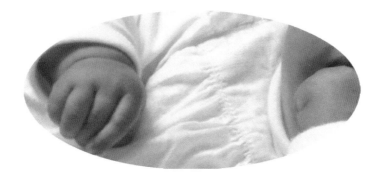

An everyday miracle - small yet perfectly formed.

REBUKE TO BISHOP BERKELEY

"I see" the blind man said;
The lamp-post dumbly stood
Insolent or impassive…

The Buddhist calmly chants
Oblivious to all
Twixt life and death.

Numb lepers lose their fingers
Deaf ears an easy victim make
Rotten smells send out a warning
Bitter tastes a poisoned lake.

Warriors meanwhile, senses shrieking
Stalk the mammoth tank.
Distraction tactics, awe-filled plan,
Whispered orders, sudden action.

(Those who survive, it's no surprise,
Feel the danger, keep their lives.)

'"I see", said the blind man to the lamp-post'

Bishop Berkeley was an early proponent of the 'Matrix' - like belief that 'we only perceive the tree in the quadrangle' by Gods' will. The tree itself 'only continues to exist when nobody is there, simply because God is an infinite mind that perceives all'.

Newtonian and Darwinian theories imply that objective reality came first, with our senses as adaptations to it.

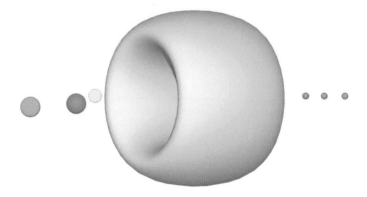

To the eye of topology,
A mere doughnut we may be.
Begin to study biology
There's a whole lot more to see.

In our body many organs
Carry out their silent functions
Hidden liver, secret spleen,
Daily do their work unseen

And unaided.... Just one
Has to serve for everyone.
What of kidneys may you ask?
What purpose they in life's repast?

I know not but others do,
Why we all have kidneys two
But if **ever one disfunction**,
Having two's great consolation.

Whether blocked or bad or both
(And to lose either you'd be loth),
Still at least our Barry'd be,
Then a man with one kidney.

So get well soon! Your health renew.
May your strength once more accrue.
Bid the nurses sweet adieux
Come back fit both through and through.

*(a poem for cousin Barry, hospitalized with renal problems.
He still has two kidneys to his name.)*

LIFE ON EARTH - 1979

Count annual rings to make a start
Dendrochronology's no mean art
Good years, bad years, many things
Can be found in annual rings

But for scope and breadth of vision
Switching on our television
Nothing matched the joy and awe
When the young Attenborough

On mule-back down the Colorado
Travelled where we'd all like to go
Each downward step a thousand years
Of the Grand Canyons' jagged tears

Geology for all to see
Living Earth's life history

David Attenborough's seminal 1979 natural history series illustrated the evolution of life in 13 episodes from single cells in program one to "The Compulsive Communicators" - ourselves.

The Grand Canyon is 1 mile deep through undisturbed sedimentary rocks

Whale-backed hills rolled past
As we approached
That place where the Earth's skin
Crumpled and flared in geologic time
Ages gone.

Camped in the green of the valley
Drew water from the stream
Surrounded by majesty.
Majesty.

Picked our way up stony paths
Past strewn and rubbled rocks
To where the land is harder, steeper, ripped.
The snow line.

Ever upwards we rose
While around us in the clear air
The mountains opened up
Like the petals of a flower
Unfolded.

Stone now great, swelling, sculptured
Caressed by our hand
While below us a jewelled lake
Ultramarine with a thousand ripples
Sparkled so bright.

See Oeschinen Lake for an example

THE SHOPPERS' LAMENT

Oh the crooks and the cranks they will sell us snake oil
Nutritional supplements in bottles and jars
Cardboard packed quiches roasted in their foil
Salt-laden snacks going cheap at the bar.

The beef at our butcher is factory fed dross
All laced up with hormones and mad cow disease
Antibiotic resistance to lessen the cost
Methane emissions thrown in just for free.

The fat in the chip-shop comes up to the boil
Fish dunked in batter browns in a broil
MacDonalds can sell us some doughy white buns
Fit for to build up our lardy white tums.

Those tasty green beans, flown in from Peru
Our fruit's boxed in plastic, a film on top too
Child labour has picked the leaf tips for our tea
Ethical consumers can we ever be?

Cosmetics section at our local supermarket

(A pale imitation of 99 Cent II Diptychon by Andreas Gursky)

HITTING A CENTURY

Captain Tom
You struggle on
Tho your back be bent
Your body racked
Still you struggle on.

You were not a man of war
When the call came,
But did not flinch
A lifetime ago, in your full strength,
To do your duty.

Those medals on your chest
No tawdry tin, but
Mementos of those glory days
When you stood ramrod straight,
Looked at Fear right in the eye and
Stared it out of countenance.

Time has turned the screw
As for all it surely must
Your body a mere broken husk.
But still you carry bravely on.

Our heart is twisted, touched,
That yours still beats so strong.
We salute you, Captain Tom
May you forever soldier on.

In 2020, aged 99, Captain Tom Moore decided to walk 100 laps of his back garden to raise £1,000 for the NHS. The media picked up on the story, with the result that by the time of his 100th birthday on 30th April, over £32Mn had been raised. Awards and accolades followed. He died 2nd February 2021.

SNAPSHOTS OF THE PAST - A HAIKU

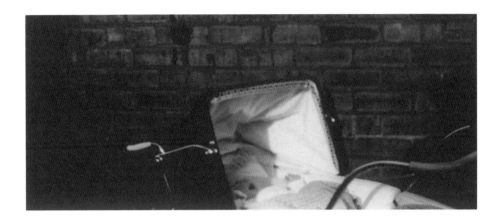

All those old photos,
Pasty faces, grimy streets.
Yesterdays forever grey.

In Japan all the world is exceedingly tight
No room to do wrong, just stick with what's right
Carefully measured, not cut to waste
Neatness in all things, each is in place.

Organization's the key to success
Work done with pride means you give of your best.
Respect for your neighbour you show at all times
Honour your elders and all of the blest.

Each train arriving perfectly on time
Passengers waiting calmly in line.
Beauty in all things, exquisite pleat,
Each tree a bonsai, manicured and complete.

Learn to be happy, learn to take part,
To love every task and to treat it as art.
Bow to your waiter, bow at the lift -
Bow on the phone, it won't go amiss!

Say please and thank you whatever you do
Arigato Gosaimatsu.

A stationery shop in Japan.

*'Arigato Gosaimatsu' is the Japanese equivalent of 'Thank you'. People say 'Arigato Gosaimatsu' **(all eight syllables)** at every possible occasion. The equivalent in English would be to continually say 'Thank you so very much indeed'.... Suburban buses say it, pre-recorded, at each and every stop.*

MASADA

It was two thousand years ago
Judaea under Roman rule
Jewish people all aglow...
Dreams of freedom fanned the fuel.

They rose up, but their rebellion failed
Romans they destroyed the Ark
Jewish tears to no avail
Of the Temple now no mark.

In Masada's fortress only strong
Rebels still they held their stand.
Below, the soldiers many thronged
Tasked to rub out all the band

On three sides the rocks fell plumb
But, to westward was a spur.
And so was ordered a great ramp
Masada for to scale by war.

Legions laboured month on month
Each rock on one man's back
Half a mountain heaved by hand
Masada to attack.

The defenders knew their time had come.
Outnumbered were they ten to one
Now that every single hope was gone
They could but go while still free men.

A suicide pact they all did make
One thousand living souls
Each trusty twenty lives to take
Reporting back to die as well.

- The chief at last by his own hand -

Two women only hid away
Left to tell the tale
That'll never be forgot
Masada remember well.

This tale has lived two thousand years
T'will live ten thousand score.
Each Jewish child a pilgrim is
Remembering evermore.

Near Masada at dawn

Walking up the Roman approach ramp.

THE HOLOCAUST

What's the worst crime in the book?
Laws and customs all agree
It's murder, murder in the first degree
To deliberately, violently bring
Another's life to a full stop.
Turn flesh to clay before its time
A living person limed in slime.

Turn these pages and you'll see
One hundred thousand dots.
Mothers, fathers, daughters, sons.
Murdered in foul conspiracy
Bludgeoned, starved, hanged and shot
The most they gassed in batches.
Herded naked into the oven.
Entombed in poison as if fishes
There to gasp their last.

Turn again, and eight times more.
And now you've hit a million
No weakness now, turn ten times more
And forty times again for luck.
Six million in living memory
Murdered most foul.

ROGER FRANÇOIS VILA

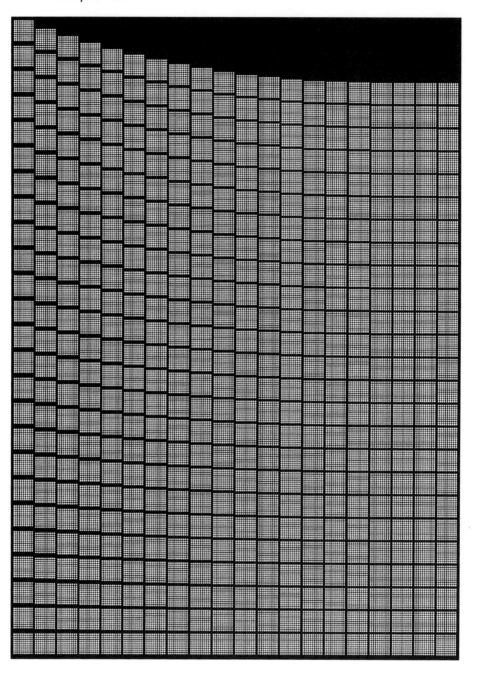

58

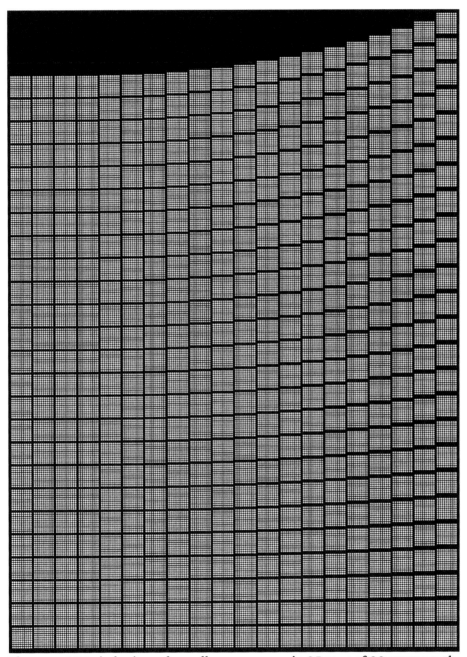

There are 100 circles in each small square group, in 25 rows of 20 groups each. So, on each page are 50,000 circles representing murdered men, women and children. To see as many circles as there were Jewish holocaust victims you have to view both pages 60 times.

A strange old man,
With beard sewn through with copper wire
(stitched under the skin)
Visited me once.

Upon my table lay by chance
A black and tattered cardboard box
Small, and stamped with silver paint.

He asked to see the contents.
The lid flipped open, revealed
A broken pocket watch and chain
For which he offered £60.

I of course refused,
For if that trinket had a worth,
Who knew what it might be?
At which he told a tale of cock and bull,
Of princes, prophecies, nations fates,
Said he'd shoot me dead should I refuse.

Gathering the box at a chance distraction,
I jumped up, made it out the door,
And fled. He in hot pursuit,
Winged me at first,
Then, catching up,
Relieved me of the box, muttered
"You know too much"
And shot me dead.

At which I woke afright.
I hope it's not a prophesy....
Should perchance it come to pass,
You know whom you should seek.

Geologic time is time so deep,
Scotland's mass like cream on coffee
Travelling at fingernail's creep
Floating on currents from Earth's core,

Waltzed unchecked for twenty thousand miles.
(Mere millimeters each and every week)
Then crashed in ultra slow mo crush
Into Europe.
....
The crumple zone is there to see,
Great alternate lines of loch and mount,
Diagonal folds a country's width
Faults and crack lines there to count.

With everywhere the frozen lumps
Of volcanoes and of lava floes
That flared and glowed those years ago
Now worn to granite stumps and crags
By ice ages scraping great swathes
Which since have gone away.
....
Four hundred million years since then have gone
But still around us change persists
Rivers dig at valley twists
Seas knaw and chumble stones to sand
Ice splits rocks for trees to grow
And over all the wind still blows

While underneath our very feet
The earth's core still is swirling
Stones still groaning lava flowing
Ready yet to dance some more.

*Here are some rocks near Stranraer in Western Scotland
that have been tilted to the vertical.*

*Geologic time was first conceived of by a Scottish geologist, James Hutton.
We now know that between roughly 425 and 390 million years
ago, Laurentia crashed into Baltica, then Avalonia, crumpling the
rock formations that today form Scotland. The process is called
the Caledonian Orogeny and is typical of plate tectonics.
… India is similarly currently impacting into Asia, with the Himalayas
as the modern crumple zone.*

If every year of your whole life
Was a second in a movie
One hundred years of love and strife
Two minutes if you're lucky.

Now if the worlds' story were played back
At the same scale,
From first big bang until today
You'd have had to start in 1600
- Galileo in his prime.

Victoria sat upon the throne
When Earth and Sun were formed…
Twelve years since Tiktaalik learned to make
The first steps onto land.
Dinosaurs great roamed five years ago.

Your meatspace life could soon be over
In not so much more time
Than you have spent to read these lines
(Let's hope a dividend is left behind)

Seconds per year = 60 per minute x 60 per hour x 24 per day x 365.25 per year
... so a scale of 1 second <> 1 year is a scale of 31,557,500 to 1.
At that scale, approximately,

Age of the Universe	430 years	<> 13,770,000,000 years
Age of the Milky Way	285 years	<> 9,000,000,000 years
Earth formation	45 years	<> 4,600,000,000 years
Life on Earth (abiogenesis)	126 years	<> 4,000,000,000 years
Tiktaalik	12 years	<> 400,000,000 years
Jurassic era	5 years	<> 170,000,000 years
Humans (Homo Sapiens)	3 days	<> 300,000 years

THE DODO AS A HAIKU

Overweight, tasty.
The Dodo was a sitting duck -
Proverbially!

Here is a rather longer version on the same lines, by Hilaire Belloc from his 'Bad Child's book of Beasts' (1896)

The Dodo used to walk around,
And take the sun and air.
The sun yet warms his native ground –
The Dodo is not there!
The voice which used to squawk and squeak
Is now for ever dumb –
Yet may you see his bones and beak
All in the Mu-se-um.

How true!

The ancestors of the Dodo and the Rodrigues solitaire diverged from the Nicobar pigeon around 23 MYA. They probably remained able to fly. Mauritius, Réunion and Rodrigues are three volcanic islands off the coast of Africa which are less than 10 million years old. Both the Dodo and Rodrigues solitaire are now extinct.

In full sunny Summer's term, within the Vale of York
We toured the solar system, a lovely country walk
It's at a scale to make you smile, each hundred meter stretch
Equals 30 million miles, no easy thing to sketch.

The Sun was held aloft on high, 8 feet across to see

100 meters off was, hi, Mercury, a large pea.

Add 90 meters, twice the size, Venus, cloudy white
Like Earth, plus global warming, as hot as molten lead.

Soon we came to our own selves,
the Earth and Moon so dear
260 meters from the sun,
so far and yet so near.

Mars followed, coloured all in red,
the next in our small set,

After which there came asteroids (mere dust specks underfoot)

Next travelled on for one more click, Jupiter at our side
A handball at the present scale,
red spot a blotch that's two Earths wide.

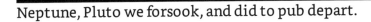

Saturn yet another click, with rings an LP's size
Made of chunks of water ice, and paper thin – no lies.

Uranus was our turning point, at five clicks from the start

Neptune, Pluto we forsook, and did to pub depart.

But if we'd tried to reach the stars,
Alpha Centauri come to soon,
We'd have 40,000 miles to scan,
a fifth-way to the moon!

*The York Astrocampus is at a scale of 575,872,239 to 1, so 100
metres along the track <> 57 million kilometres in space.*

*The word 'kilometer' is deeply unpoetic, hence the army term 'click' rather than
km. More information: https://astrocampus.york.ac.uk/cycle-the-solar-system/*

Visitor car parking is available at Askham Bar Park & Ride, off A1036, YO23 2BB

The photos are more or less at the same scale: approximately: Sun, diameter 1,394,900km <> 892 pixels (nearly a page wide)

Mercury, diameter 4,880km <> 3 pixels on the page. The orbit of Mercury is elliptical, between 46 and 69 $10^{\wedge 6}$ km, so Mercury is between 33 and 49 pages away from the Sun at this scale.

Venus, diameter 12,100km <> 7 pixels (77 pages away on average)

Earth, diameter 12,740km <> 8 pixels (107 pages...)

Mars, diameter 6,800km <> 4 pixels (163 pages...)

Jupiter, diameter 71,500km <> 45 pixels (557 pages...)

Saturn, diameter 120,500km <> 77 pixels (1027 pages...)

Uranus, diameter 51,000km <> 32 pixels (2060 pages...)

THE WINDMILLS HAIKU

Majestic white wings
Perfect circles scythe so smooth
Harvesting our skies

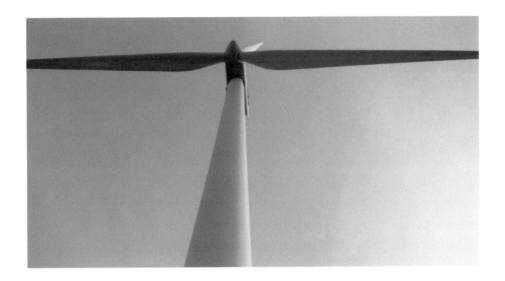

DREAM OF FISH ON A PLANE

We had two fish upon our plane,
Fresh-caught,
Lying on the cabin floor
And still alive.

Uncertain what to do with them,
We flew on,
When suddenly one fish of the two
Scuttled on its legs or fins
To behind an instrument panel.

I thought it was a Gudgeon
But it could have been a Lungfish
Now what to do we asked ourselves
Kill the other while we had the chance?

One thing we knew for sure, that dead fish stink.
- Dead or alive both had to go!

It was actually a Periophthalmus novemradiatus, a mudskipper.
*A better suited specimen would have been a Tiktaalik (the ancestor of amphibians,
reptiles, birds and mammals) but as these lived about 375 million years ago,
any antics by them on a plane would be a bit anachronistic.*

KEEPING UP WITH THE JONESES

Our neighbour's bought a Tesla
Sleek and black and scary fast
Maybe we should get another
Petrol engine's days now past.

Then like two great racing cougar
On sunny kerbside they will bask
Waiting to chase one after t'other
Jones or us two - who'd be last?

A CELEBRATION - 2020 VERSION

Were I a genii or a djinn
From Ali Baba's basket newly raised
Or some great magician
A sage by others greatly praised

A prophecy would I make
As plague did rage across the strand,
That for your birthday's sake
- Prohibitions not withstand -

You shall,

Easily and at your command,
Cleansed beyond belief, by magic carpet carried
Travel to feast on food from foreign land,
By chefs deliciously prepared

Then return to the playing
Of sweet music all in tune

This would happen for the queen
May quite soon it all be seen.

*It was between first and second lockdowns, so we drove
into town and ate at a French Restaurant...*

THE PIANO-TUNER

Our piano had a heart of gold
And sang out with good cheer
But sounded more like honky-Tonk
Befugged by too much beer.

His driver supped on cups of tea
With small talk made pastime
His guide dog waiting patiently
Sat quiet, made no sign.

Intent the mindful expert worked
Note by note brought home
The magic elixir uncorked
The word turned into poem.

Each tone now endowed with grace,
Subtlety, and the light
Of a thousand shining spheres.
Each scales' silky ripple
A testament to his skill.
Sweet music, up lifted delight.

We thanked him and we paid his fee
It was not too much to ask
Our piano now for all to see
Endowed enhanced and blest.

A ROLLING STONE

When we're young, at last set free
A rolling stone we want to be
Give me motion, let it be,
That there grows no moss on me.

Roll the years but a bit more
And we ask what freedom's for
When the gushing rush of life
Is eased, then we seek less strife.

We settle for a bed to lie in
With a nice round smooth companion
Who fits us well. Draw up the moss!
Freedom's not so great a loss.

Make two more souls. Once we're four,
Time for them to roll some more.

Wind-blown trash they glumly gather
At bus-stop and by back street corner
Puffa jacket, tracksuit, sneakers,
Fitly clothed for ever leisure.

Pasty face and sagging bum
Lardy guts that weigh a ton.
What's the point their hopeless motto
I give up their sad refrain.

Unemployment can be very hard to live with...

SINNERS REPENT!

Smokers
In their hand is clasped a fag
Defiantly they draw a good deep drag
Inhale the drug into their lung
Turn soft flesh to greying scum.

Ignore the warnings, thrice repeated
Forget the fear of cancer near
It's not my fault should lightning strike
But here and now, I need a light

Boozers
Boozy happy, boozy drunk,
You don't know how fast you're sunk
Raucous mirth and songs you utter
Then spew up into the gutter.

Now look on with yellowed eye
As the light in you does die.
Liver jaundiced, pancreatic
From too many times palatic.

Druggies
See him lie in lethargy
Could end up at A and E
Sunken eyes and hollow cheeks
Hasn't had a meal for weeks

Lit a fire of ecstasy
Will burn out to misery
Must rekindle at all cost
Until all that's left is lost.

Gamblers
Seek the thrill adrenaline

What was yours may now be mine
Casino pusher takes his cut
Drip by drip to cop the lot.

The Moral
Mens sana, corpore sano
Healthy body with mind will go
Show a leg and shine a light
That's the way of honour bright.

Keep your habits true and pure
Kind and useful, right for sure.

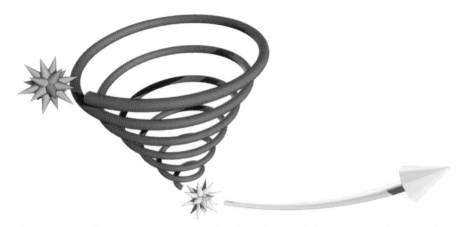

Relapse triggers often set off the downwards spiral of an addiction... but a trigger event can sometimes break it.

Fair words, measured claims built up
Grievance backlogged upon resentment
Immovable earth imbued with force
Awaits the catalyst.

Suddenly released tsunami crash
Sweeps all before it.
Spillicans in the storm.
Tortured parturition.

Is every nation born in pain?
Must innocent blood every cause bedeck?
Do only martyrs mothers screams resound?
Will tribal instincts ever end?

Irish nationalists seized the Dublin G.P.O building during the 1916 Easter Rising. It has now been restored, with a museum in the basement, the entrance to which is on the right in the photo.

SUMO HAIKU

Man-mountain action
Shocking crunch explosive force
Only one can win.

Sumo wrestler preparing for the fight. When it starts the action is surprisingly fast and decisive.

Miraculous birth -
Life a complex comedy,
Death the final sleep.

THE QUARREL

Not again
You never
I can't stand it
What about?

I didn't say that you hadn't said that I couldn't

Lovers bicker amongst endless negatives

GOOOOGLE

When Sergei Brin and Larry Page
Page-rankings first devised
Bright-eyed students, idealful
Could scarce have e'er surmised

That within a mere short score of years
They'd scoop the world both eyes and ears
In laptop and handheld device
Unstoppably and 'at no price'.

Map every road and cycle path
To take us surely home to hearth.
Now, fit use for such great wealth
They teach the car to drive itself!

While others searched the Net in vain,
To émigré, global domain.

Sergey Brin's parents emigrated to the US from the USSR in 1979
when he was six years old. Larry Page and he met while they were
both studying for PhDs in Computer Science at Stanford U.

GLEN COE

Moor of Rannoch, blasted heath,
Strewn with rock pools, witches brew
Gives way at end to dark Glen coe
Of wicked history still now new.

Where clan Campbell, forever cursed
Broke every bound of bare humanity
Their host MacDonalds murdered as they slept.

We of course care not a whit
We come for youthful fresh-faced fun
In February amidst the snow
Adventure there to come.
Up giant sisters shoulders climb
The jagged Aonach Egach ridge to find.

One simple slip is all it takes
Wet boot, wet rock, minor mistake.
The void beckons, slow motion...
Totter helpless, helpless slide
Gravity untrammelled,
Sudden blow.
Run the gauntlet, bones a broken
Come to rest a bloody lump
There to freeze and thaw betimes.

But not to us. We make it safe
Returning down the Devils Stairs
With dusk slow shading into darkness,
Tired but triumphant. A good weekend.

THE COSMIC BOOKCASE

If every year since space and time
First were cracked asunder
Was chronicled by a page
(Double sided if you please)
One ream five hundred years would span
Take us back to Leonardo in his prime
A hefty tome but one of many –
Two reams per thousand years.

Let's place them on a shelf
The last of a long line
Since matter first began to build
The great empire now around us.

Every meter length of shelf
Ten thousand years in the making.
Ten millennia passed in one long stride.

But how long the shelf?
To the birth of sapiens us,
About a million years, a hundred meters,
To death of dinosaurs, sixty times that,
Let's say four miles.

A hundred times more since living slush
First bloomed and splashed
Upon an ocean shore, not long since that star dust
Coalesced, aggregated,
Into our sun and planets home.

Near Land's End to John O'Groats
Since with first bang our universe
- Space, time, matter, energy -
Went nuclear, sprang wide open

Now look on.
The library of time
Is still half empty!
Rows shelve
Off into the future. Hazy yes,
But here the death of our dear sun
Some three hundred miles along
By which time we hope
Our avatars have reached a star
To warm their virtual circuits -
Or even packed a spaceship
Full of meat and of two veg
Deep freezer fresh and
Off to pastures new.

An end of time?
The jury's out
Does cosmos crunch or freeze at last?
Or maybe loop the loop or bounce?
Fifteen billion years or so hence
On shelving stretched a thousand miles to fit
The story's end may then be writ.

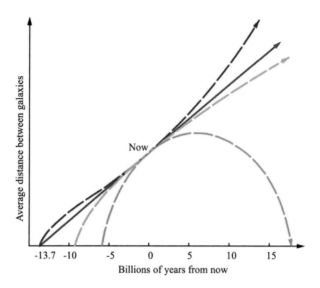

The jury is still out on what the end state is. This graph based on "Solutions of the Friedman Equations (not hand drawn)" by Ben RG.   See the 'Ultimate fate of the universe'. Idea of using a sheet of A4 paper per year taken from Dawkins, Richard, 'Unweaving The Rainbow'

Translucent, evanescent, luminous and so pure
All colours unwoven by each raindrop's sphere
Spread out in an arc cross cloud, over hill
A million raindrops they are all falling still.

We need no more to talk of miracle
Or pots full of gold, leprechauns for to fill
But still spirits lift up when across sky's face
A rainbow is stretched as if by God's grace.

A hose in the garden can make for our joy
A rainbow, to order, any sunny day
But like conjurors' so neat little ploy
The raindrops from heaven they are hidden away.

Unpredictable jewelled sparkle that all do enjoy
Alluring enchanting for each man and boy....

*This poem can be sung as if to the hymn Immortal, invisible, God only
wise, originally a Welsh ballad tune, "Can mlynedd i nawr" ("A Hundred
Years from Now"), adapted for church use in 1839.*

When Galileo had his day
And history proved him right
The Earth a planet of the sun,
Itself a shining star...

Like those above that you could count
Some seven thousand more.

The mind of man took quite a bump
But there were more in store.
The silky scarf of Milky Way
A trillion suns comprised -

And not so very long ago
They were a bit surprised.

In depths of space at edge of ken
Those reddish smudges hard to see
Were trillions yet more galaxies
Far beyond the reach of men.

With a teaspoon in your hand
Go down to nearest beach.
Take one heaped teaspoon of sand
And spread it on a sheet.

In the sky they now have found
As many stars as grains of sand
One each and every beach around
On planet Earth in every land.

A teaspoonful of sand

A trillion is 10^{12} and there are 10^{12} stars in the average galaxy with about 10^{12} galaxies, making the number of stars in the observable universe currently around 10^{24}, "more stars than all the grains of sand on Planet Earth", as Carl Sagan used to say.

By the way, Galileo was not the first person to have thought of the heliocentric model of the world. This is credited by Archimedes to Aristarchus of Samos. On the basis of stellar parallax Archimedes guessed the diameter of the Universe to be about 2 light years. On this basis, with a 0.019mm diameter grain of sand, he calculated in his paper 'The Sand Reckoner' that it would take 10^{63} grains of sand to fill the universe.

The geocentric theory of Aristotle and Ptolemy was preferred by the church, but the knowledge of the heliocentric model was not lost. Nicolaus Copernicus attributed the heliocentric model to Aristarchus. Copernicus in his turn influenced Galileo, whose telescopic observations proved the point.

CAMOUFLAGE

What lucky species are we,
Top dogs both at land and sea.
Proud as peacocks we can strut,
Showing off our colours bright.

The time we really have to fear,
Is when two nations are at war.
Then each hides himself away,
Secret, ready, for affray.

Thus in snow like polar bear,
Or in dust, khaki must wear
And in woodland, dappled green,
Not to feel the arrow keen.

Lest that death come from afar
From *us*, apex predator

When in a predator / prey situation, camouflage is very beneficial, with strong evolutionary pressure against individuals who stand out. There are at least as many light as dark moths in this picture.

As the Industrial Revolution got underway in England, pollution increased. No dark peppered moths were seen before 1811; by 1898 the dark moths formed 98% of the population in Manchester; with the passing of the Clean Air Act in 1956 atmospheric pollution was greatly reduced and lighter-coloured moths returned.

You can see the situation from the point of view of the predator by playing the Peppered Moth Game online (https://askabiologist.asu.edu/peppered-moths-game/play.html), from which this screenshot has been taken. Try playing a few hands to see how your score improves...

A WEDDING VOW

Forty years ago today
We stood together proud to say
We'd love each other night and day,
Stay together come what may.

Forty years can come to pass
Before we each do breathe our last,
But with my very final gasp
I'll say "I love you", slow and fast.

And if no future then we know
Down on Earth our love will glow...
Children's children glad to grow
From those seeds that love did sow.

So let's rejoice and happy be
Joined at the hip! eternally.

When they write the big red book
Of this our latest century
Let's hope it's plain for all to see
That man the path of wisdom took

That coal fires all are long put out
A child of five self-drives to school
Still networking with friends not cruel
While rockets land without a shout

That all of planet Earth is mine
And yours, and his, and hers, and ours
To cherish rather than to devour
As race and nation full entwine

That it's all a big success story
And wars are ancient history.

A future Spacex Falcon Heavy landing (based on the 2019 twin landing).

POSTSCRIPT

In the spirit of Natural Selection, this anthology contains three more poems than the 52 that are described in the title.

Readers who have made it to this point are welcome to suggest which poems they would like to see culled....

Please email postmaster@simulations.plus.com with your hitlist, together with any other comments which may come to mind.